YOUR LITTLE SLEEP

An illustrated storybook
for children having
an operation or scan
under general anaesthesia

Written and Illustrated by
Dr Ann-Marie Crowe

in association with

Sláinte Leanaí Éireann

CHI

Children's Health Ireland

This book is an official resource of the
College of Anaesthesiologists of Ireland
and the Royal College of Surgeons in Ireland.

This project received development funding from the
HSE Spark Innovation Programme 2020.

Design by Nolan Book Design

About the Book

This book is written and illustrated by a doctor working in a children's hospital. It aims to explain to children the process involved in coming into hospital for an operation or scan that requires general anaesthesia. It introduces children to some of the people they will encounter during their hospital visit and outlines what will happen when they are there.

This book can be read aloud to a younger child (children aged 5–6), or read by a child (independent readers aged 7–10) in their own time in advance of their hospital visit. Children older than 10 years of age may also find this book helpful in their preparation.

Although this book is targeted at children aged 5 years and older, some younger children may engage with the story and the illustrated characters featured in the book nonetheless.

Hello!

My name is **Annie** and I'm a **doctor** in the hospital.

I'm here to tell you about what happens if you ever need to come to **hospital** for an operation or a scan.

I'll tell you all about my exciting job, who you will meet when you are in hospital and how you might feel when you are here!

Can I tell you all about it?

To get ready for the day, you will have to fast – this means you won't have anything to eat for a few hours!

When you **skip breakfast** or have a really early breakfast, you might feel a little hungry. You can have something to eat once the operation or scan is over!

You can **drink water**, so you won't be thirsty! Do you know who else likes to drink water? Can you see him in the picture?

He looks hungry!

You might want to **pack a bag** at home to help you get ready for your hospital visit. Have you a **favourite book or toy** that you'd like to bring with you?

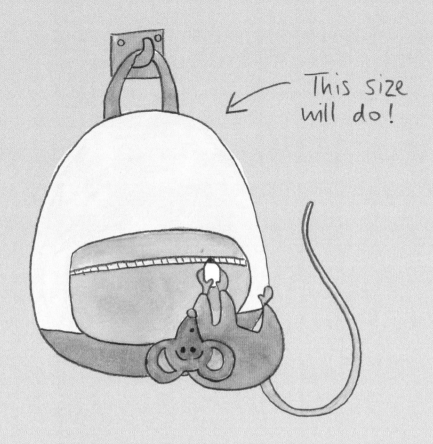

If you have to stay in hospital overnight, you won't need to bring a lot of things!

Packing your toothbrush and some clothes is a good idea!

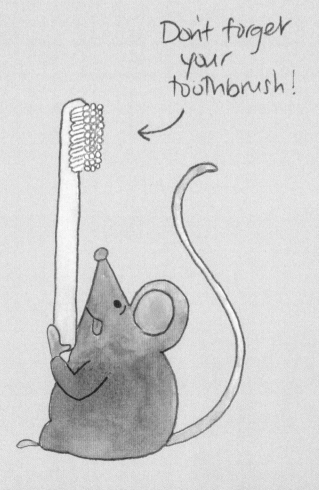

The hospital is a **really big building** – much bigger than crèche or school!

It's a **busy place** and is full of nice people who are happy to see you. They will **look after you** while you are here!

There are lots of ways to travel to the hospital – by **car**, **bus**, **train**. Maybe you live close enough to **walk**! I usually **cycle** into work! Can you see my bicycle?

My bicycle

My Hospital badge

My Bicycle helmet

HOSPITAL

When you arrive at the hospital,
you will **check in** at a desk.
This means that your
parent will tell us
that you have arrived
so that we can get
ready to meet you!

Nurse

After you have checked in, a **friendly nurse** will meet you and give you a **plastic bracelet** to wear on your wrist. This bracelet will have your name on it!

The nurse will ask you to stand or sit on a weighing scales to check your **weight**.

There will be a **hospital chart** just for you. The doctors and nurses will write all about your hospital stay in the chart!

Charts

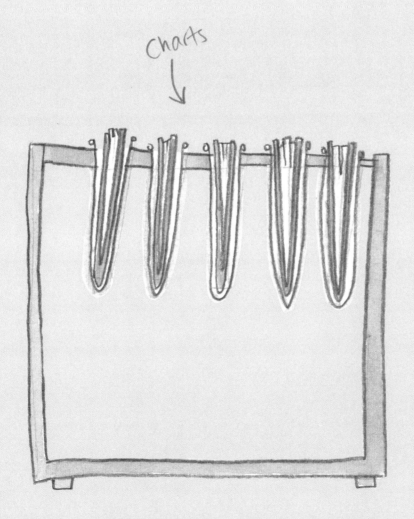

All around the hospital, you will notice lots of **hand sanitiser dispensers** and **sinks with soap**.

Hand sanitiser is a liquid that you rub between your hands. It keeps your hands nice and clean – just like soap!

Hand sanitiser

sink

Washing your hands helps stop the spread of germs –
so **it's really important to wash your hands!**

I wash my hands when I come into work, and several
times throughout the day! **Can you show me how
you wash yours?**

Thankfully, it doesn't take as long as having a shower
or a bath – **washing your hands is really easy**!

If you're having an **operation**, you will meet the **surgeons** after you get checked in. The surgeons are doctors who carry out operations in hospital. You might remember meeting them at an appointment or when you were in the emergency department!

Surgeons often wear **scrubs**, which look very like pyjamas, even though they are at work!

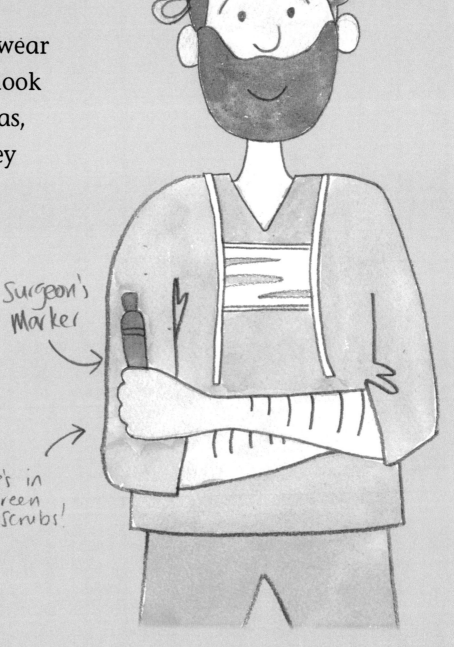

Blue hat

Surgeon's marker

He's in green scrubs!

They will **talk to you** about the operation and will answer any questions that you might have!

They will **examine** you before the operation and might draw on your skin with a **special marker** – this will rub off after the operation!

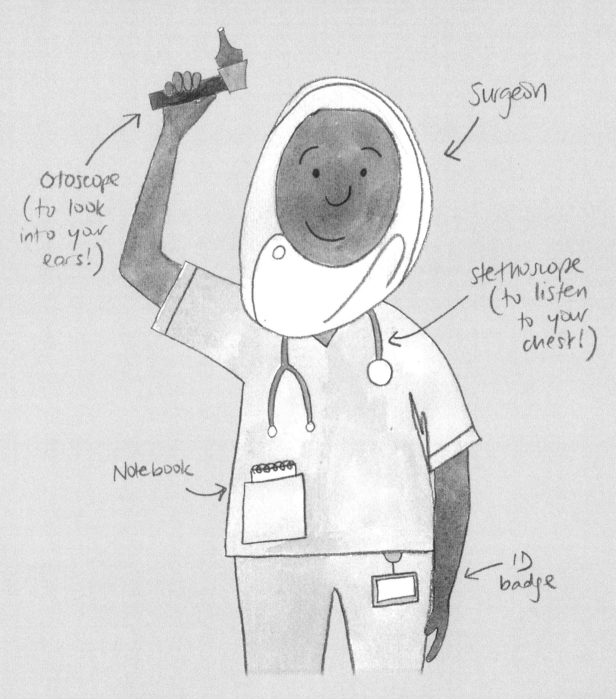

Sometimes you might not be having an operation. Instead, you might be getting a **scan**.

A scan is a very **special photograph** that takes a look at the inside of your body! A big machine takes the photograph – I think it looks like a **spaceship**! What do you think it looks like?

This takes the special photograph!

Your pillow!

While you're waiting for the operation or scan, a nurse might put some **magic cream** on the back of your hand or on the inside of your elbows.

It's **soft** and **squidgy**, a bit like an octopus that tickles!

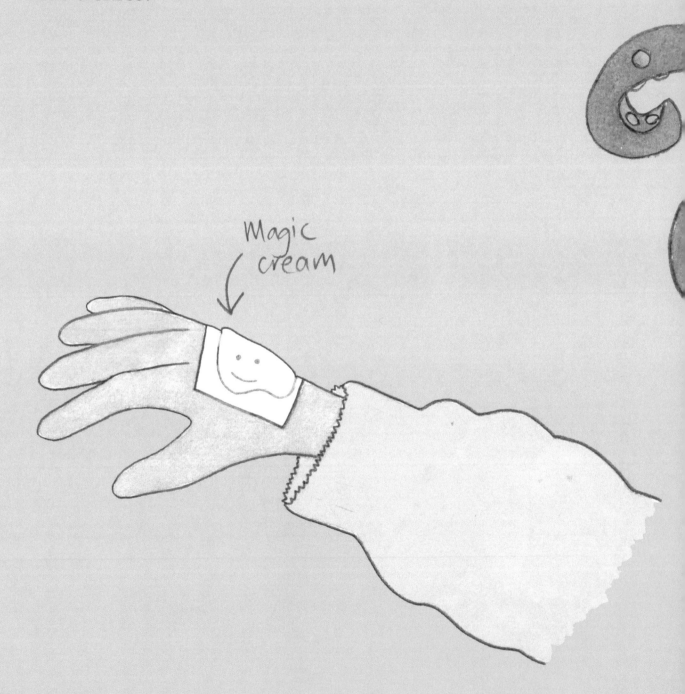

Magic cream

your
drink!

You might also be given a **drink** before you go to
theatre. This drink helps you feel calm and relaxed
– it's in a small cup and you have to drink it quickly!

Well done!

You might get a **cannula** before you come to theatre.

"Cannula" means little straw, but we call it a **Freddie**! Have you had a Freddie before?

The magic cream is useful for when you get a Freddie – it makes your skin soft and comfortable!

Arm band (this comes off!)

When you get a Freddie, a small **arm band** is put across your arm above your elbow.

Then a nurse or a doctor will **gently slide** the tiny straw into your hand. This might feel like a little pinch, or you might not feel anything at all!

It all stays in place with a special **sticker**. Can you see Freddie in the picture?

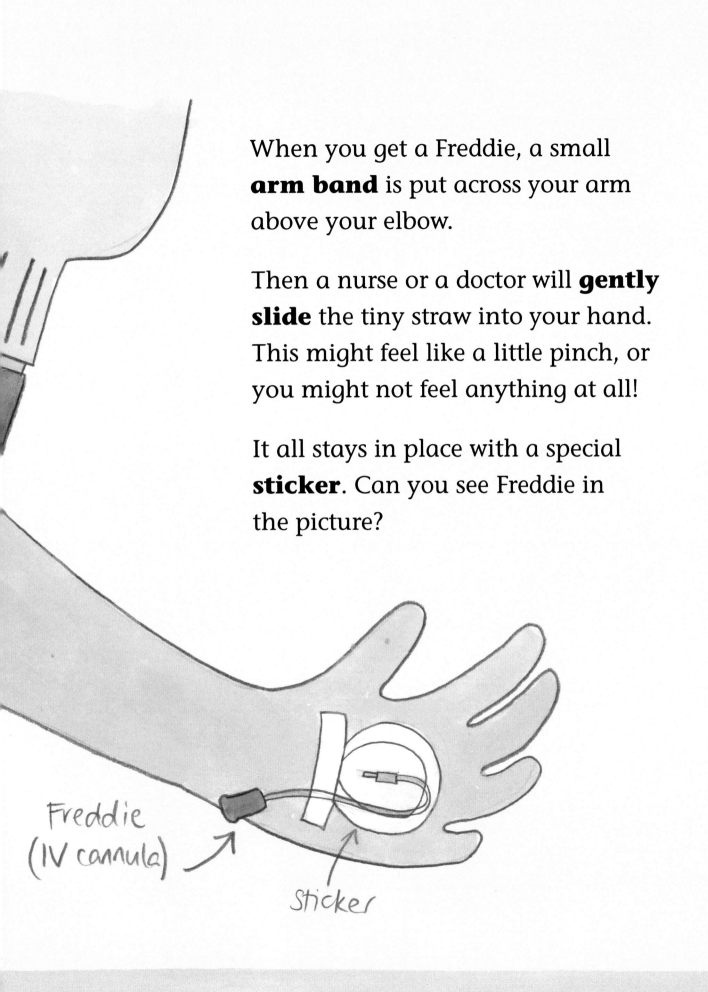

Freddie
(IV cannula)

Sticker

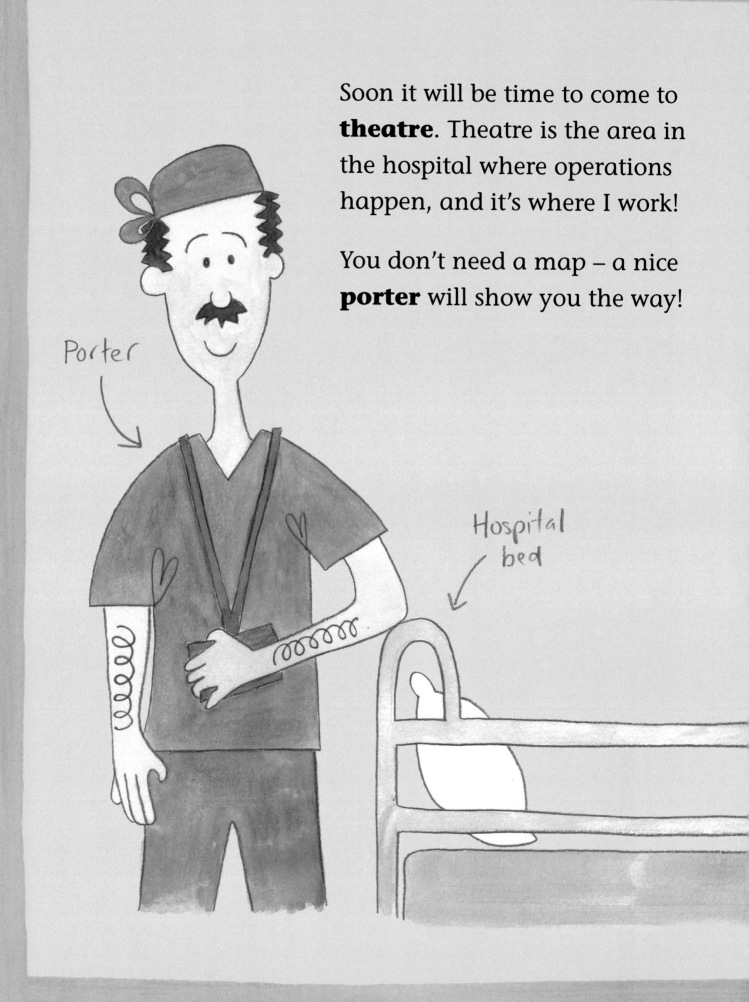

Soon it will be time to come to **theatre**. Theatre is the area in the hospital where operations happen, and it's where I work!

You don't need a map – a nice **porter** will show you the way!

Porter

Hospital bed

Another **nurse** will check your bracelet and your chart, then you'll come into the room where I work – this is the part that I look forward to!

Anaesthetic nurse

Like I said before, I am a doctor in the hospital. I'm a special kind of doctor called an **anaesthesiologist**.

Can you try saying that?

Ann-as-thee-see-oll-oh-jist.

Good work!

You can call me a **sleepy doctor**.

I make it possible for you to have an operation or scan by giving you some **sleepy medicine** that will help you fall into a **special**, **deep sleep**. You won't feel a thing and you will stay asleep the entire time.

I will look after you when you are asleep and will **wake you up** when it's all over!

I wear **scrubs** (like the surgeon) and I always look forward to meeting you!

Sometimes, I might have to wear an extra **face mask**, **visor**, **gloves** and **gown**, so you might only get to see my eyes. Of course, my smiling face is still there under all the layers!

You might see other doctors or nurses also wearing this special outfit – we occasionally wear it for **extra protection**.

Thankfully it's not as heavy as a suit of armour!

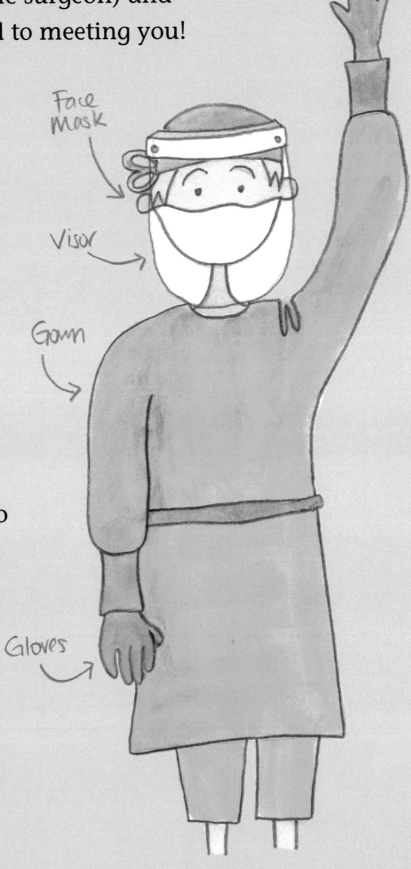

Face Mask

Visor

Gown

Gloves

slightly
heavier
outfit

When you're visiting me in theatre, I will show you the **sleep machine** and all the monitors – they're all different colours and some go **beep**, **boop**, and **ping**!

The sleep machine also has a **balloon** attached to it – can you see what colour the balloon is?

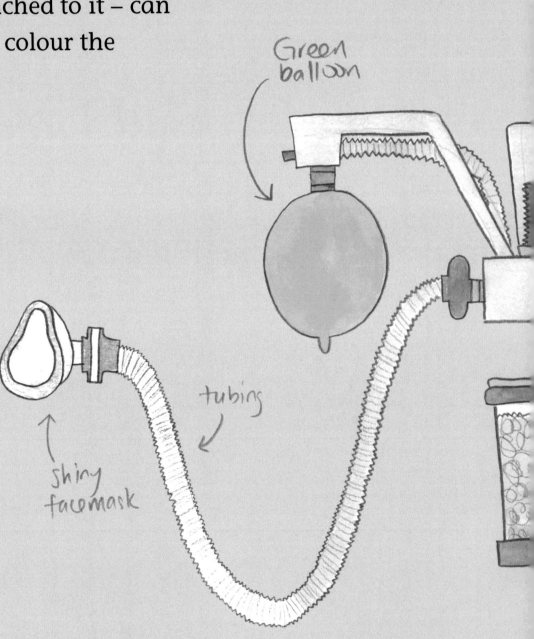

Green balloon

tubing

shiny facemask

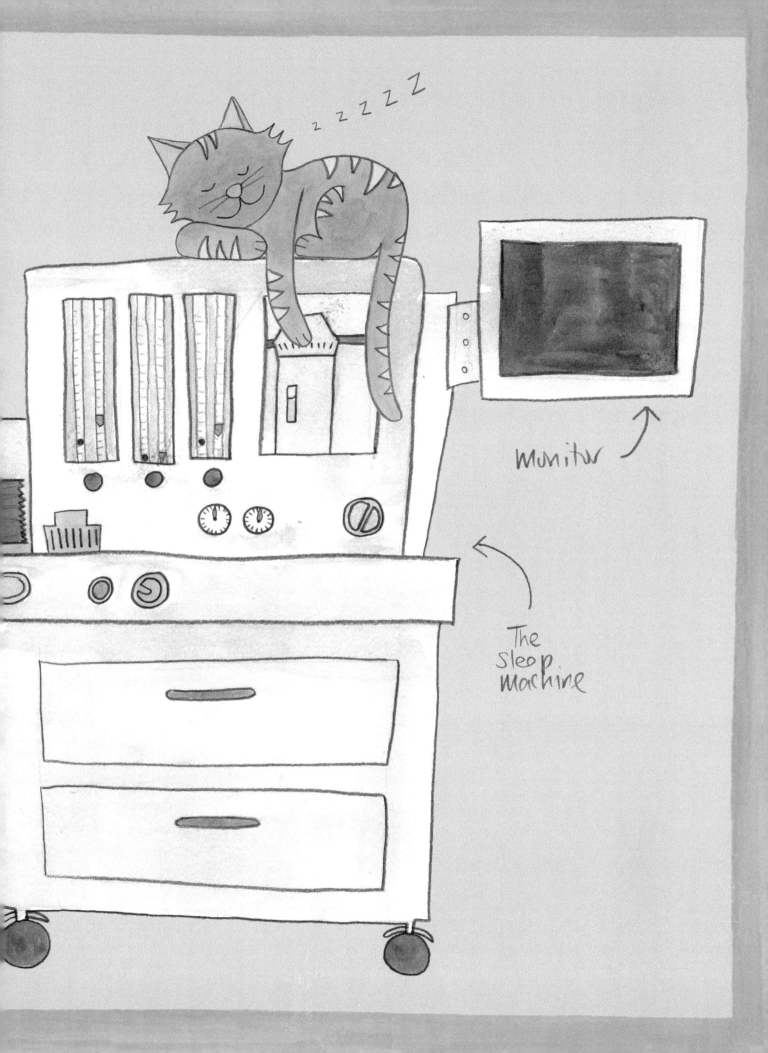

Monitor

The
Sleep
Machine

There are two different ways to get sleepy medicine.

One is to breathe in the sleepy medicine through a **clear mask** placed gently over your nose and mouth. By blowing into the shiny mask, you can **blow the green balloon up** and down.

I'll show you how to do it! Can you go **huff**, **puff**, **huff**, **puff**?? Brilliant!

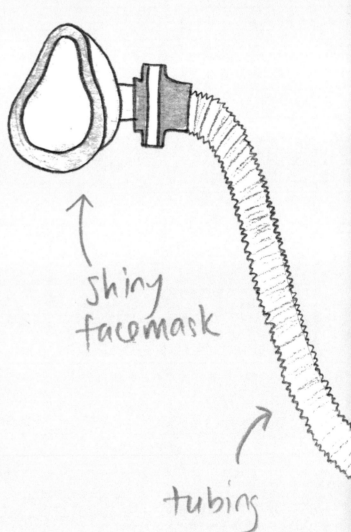

shiny facemask

tubing

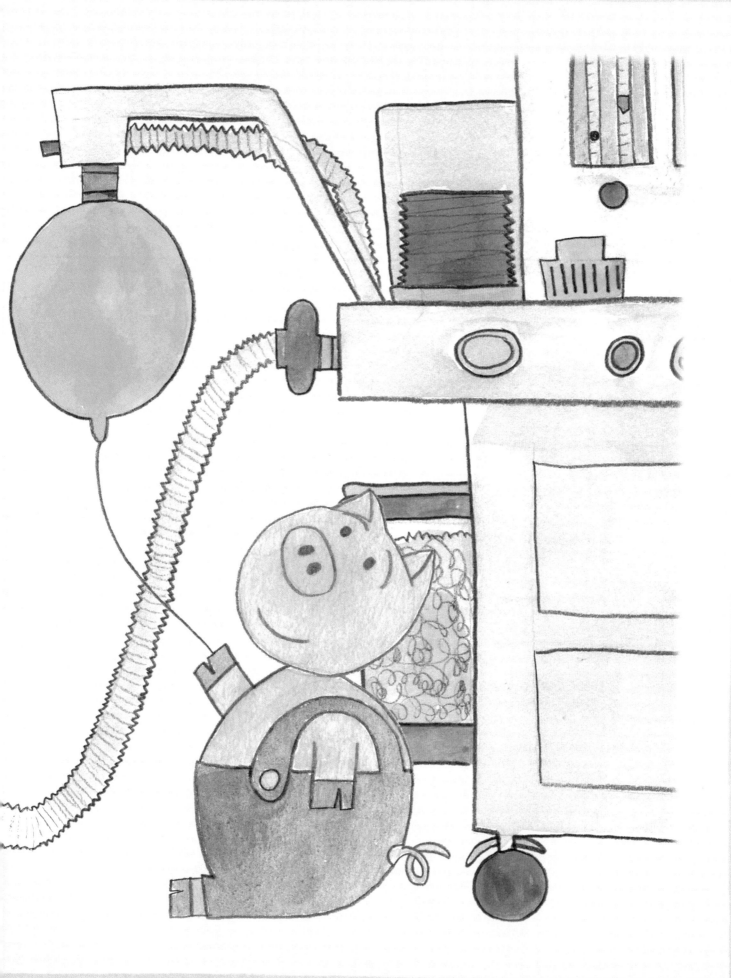

The other way to get the sleepy medicine is through your **Freddie**, if you have one in your hand!

Freddie can get **thirsty** in theatre! I like to drink coffee when I'm thirsty, but Freddie loves a **white**, **milky medicine** that feels a little cold – like penguin milk!

When Freddie gets a drink, you might feel the cold **sparkles** moving up your arm!

Your eyes will get heavy and you'll want to fall asleep!

I will look after you the entire time you are asleep and when your operation or scan is finished, **I will wake you up again**!

What do you think you'll **dream** about?

your pillow

Remote control

Special bed

When you wake up, a special nurse
will look after you in a big room
called the recovery room which
is close to theatre.

You might feel a little funny or tired at first, but the nurse will make sure you **feel better**, and can give you medicine if you need it! When you start to feel hungry again, you will be able to have something to **eat** and **drink**!

Your parent will be nearby and will come to see you really soon!

Before long, it will be time to go **home**. We'll be sorry to see you go, but I'm sure you will be happy to be home again!

If you have any **questions**, just ask an adult at home, or ask any of the nurses or doctors when you arrive into hospital!

Before coming in for the operation or scan, you might have lots of **different feelings**.

You might feel happy knowing your surgeon will help you get better, or you might feel scared or nervous, and this is OK.

It's a good idea to **think about how you feel** and to **talk** to your parent or an adult you trust about it. They will **listen** to you and help you prepare!

Don't forget your bag!

We are all looking forward to meeting you, and we are always **happy to talk to you about anything**!

Can you remember **everyone** you'll meet in the hospital?

Here's a picture to remind you!

About the Author and Illustrator

Ann-Marie Crowe is a doctor who is working as a paediatric anaesthesiologist in CHI Crumlin, Dublin (she's one of the sleepy doctors).

When she's not at work, she enjoys running, reading and watercolour painting!

Acknowledgements

A word of thanks to Dr Aisling Ní Cheallaigh, Senior Clinical Psychologist at CHI Crumlin, for her enthusiasm and contribution to the finalised text.

A special thanks to all hospital staff who work hard to make sure coming to theatre is an enjoyable experience for children and their parents.

Resources

The CHI Crumlin hospital website is a useful resource, which provides up-to-date information for parents and carers. It can be found at **www.olchc.ie**